T0129728

A Story of Faith and Love

ATTEN-TION!
PARADE REST

Heather Anne Porterhaus

BALBOA.
PRESS
A DIVISION OF HAY HOUSE

Balboa Press books may be ordered through booksellers or by contacting:

Balboa Press
A Division of Hay House
1663 Liberty Drive
Bloomington, IN 47403
www.balboapress.com
1 (877) 407-4847

Because of the dynamic nature of the Internet, any web addresses or links contained in this book may have changed since publication and may no longer be valid. The views expressed in this work are solely those of the author and do not necessarily reflect the views of the publisher, and the publisher hereby disclaims any responsibility for them.

The author of this book does not dispense medical advice or prescribe the use of any technique as a form of treatment for physical, emotional, or medical problems without the advice of a physician, either directly or indirectly. The intent of the author is only to offer information of a general nature to help you in your quest for emotional and spiritual well-being. In the event you use any of the information in this book for yourself, which is your constitutional right, the author and the publisher assume no responsibility for your actions.

Any people depicted in stock imagery provided by Getty Images are models, and such images are being used for illustrative purposes only. Certain stock imagery © Getty Images.

Print information available on the last page.

ISBN: 978-1-9822-0037-4 (sc)
ISBN: 978-1-9822-0038-1 (hc)
ISBN: 978-1-9822-0045-9 (e)

Library of Congress Control Number: 2018902427

Balboa Press rev. date: 03/16/2018

CONTENTS

This book is dedicated to the children
I love and raised as my own.
You brought me a great deal of joy,
Happiness and pride.
I wish you the best of everything in life.

ACKNOWLEDGMENTS

A special thanks to Cassidy Rivers. The artwork for the book cover has far exceeded my expectation. Your incredible talents are a blessing.

Ethel. Thank you for encouraging me to write this book. I love you more than you will ever know.

Several families and individuals assisted me long this journey. Telling this story is how I thank you for all the support you provided along the way. My gratitude can never be measured in earthly terms.

Our Pastor. I am grateful for you always keeping me spiritually grounded. The numerous times I felt I couldn't go any further, you gently helped me pull it all together. We are all blessed for it.

My Aunt. Without your spiritual teachings, I would have never heard God's call to open my heart and home to children in need. I hope from the realm of heaven you are smiling.

My cousins. Knowing our family meant I didn't need to explain what was going on. Your love helped to keep me going.

The many unknown sponsors. Your contributions helped turn little children into responsible young adults. My gratitude is immeasurable.

ATTEN-TION! PARADE-REST
A Story of Faith and Love

This unusual story shows how life takes unexpected events and several detours through many challenging trials. Choosing the right fork in the road can be as simple as daring to take a leap of faith listening to inner guidance. To understand how this narrative unfolds I'll start at the beginning and recount significant events as they occurred.

My earliest memories go back to age four when our family moved from Wisconsin to Indiana. This move took us to a neighborhood with plenty of children to play and attend school with. These were happy years filled with laughter and fun. My youngest siblings weren't born yet, so I spent quality time with my parents and older sister. There were several years between us and she spoiled me in every way possible. She taught me everything from tying my shoe laces to dressing myself. Teaching me to identify the colors of my crayons and learning the letters of the alphabet was a labor of love. Under her coaching I learned quickly. I was reading children's books by the time I was three years old, and legibly printing my name by four. This early education enabled mom to enroll me in kindergarten a year early. School gave me something productive to do while mom took care of our growing family.

My favorite childhood memories are of attending school and playing with the neighborhood children. After chores were finished, it was time to head outside to play. My friends and I could spend all day chasing each other playing tag, riding bikes, jumping double dutch rope, shooting marbles, and playing hopscotch. Groups of us played hide and go seek, tall trees and sheds were excellent hiding places. Cowboys and Indians was my favorite. Having a toy bow and arrow as well as a holster for my cap gun allowed me to play both roles. Using empty mayonnaise jars to catch lightening bugs and butterflies often became a competition.

Climbing the highest trees, catching ants and not being afraid of snakes or frogs, I was considered a tomboy. From my perspective the slimy multicolored scales of snakes and the moist rough bumpy skin of frogs was fascinating. One time I was dared to kiss a frog to see if it would turn into a prince. I did kiss the frog but no prince appeared. That was me, just doing my thing. We played until the street lights came on signaling it was time to get home.

At the end of a long day of playing, mom would peel off our dirt-soaked clothes and put us in a nice warm bubble bath. For my younger sister and me, the tub was another play area. We pretended to be scuba diving or seeing who could hold their breath the longest while under water. Mom would leave us there while she tended to whoever was the current baby. Eventually the water cooled and we had to leave the bathtub. With wrinkled fingers and toes, a quick brush of our hair and we were sent off to bed. As a teenager my dad had been a lifeguard at a beach along the shores of a nearby lake.

He taught us how to swim and by age four I could dive into a swimming pool without making much more than a ripple when I hit the water. Dad also did a little boxing in his youth. While my sister and I were young, he taught us the art of boxing. We were never standing close enough for punches to physically connect, he just wanted us to know the procedures without hurting each other. Before long this skill came in handy. While at play during recess a boy intentionally pushed me off the swing. He was having a belly laugh watching me fall to the ground skinning my knees. The laughter ended when he was surprised seeing me get up and punch his lights out. After school that day his parents came to our home showing my dad what I had done to their child. My dad looked at the boy then looked at me. After admiring my work he said, "good job, you got his lip and nose"! Without being aware of it I stood up to a bully and have done so ever since.

Adults kept a close watch over all the children in the neighborhood ensuring we were kept safely out of harm's way. A neighbor living on our block gave cookies to children on our way home from school. She was a wonderful elderly lady with snow white hair. Walking slowly she used a cane to steady herself and once in a while the cane made contact with the butt of an unruly child. I adored her and often stopped by to help pull weeds from her rose garden or any other chore she needed help with. All my grandparents we long gone before I was five years old, so the love and kindness of this lady became the grandmother I had always wished for.

When I was seven years old she became ill and passed away. Eavesdropping on the adult's conversation I thought I understood what happened to her. The way my young mind interrupted this situation is as follows: apparently she had been sick, passed away, was sleeping peacefully and was going home to be with the Lord. Her family and church members were having her wake at a nearby funeral home. The funeral home was where people went after they got sick. Since the service was called a "wake" I naturally assumed the church and family members would "wake" her up and she would be fine. My assumption for this was based on my lack of understanding of the word *wake* pertaining to this situation. I was often told to go and *wake* my dad or anyone else that was sleeping. Knowing they got up and were fine, I assumed the same thing would happen for her. My parents decided it was time for me to be introduced to this stage of life and allowed me to attend the services. However, no one explained the finality of death to me so my own imagination took over. I loved this lady and was excited to be there when she woke up.

Arriving at the funeral home I was shocked to see everyone dressed in black and ever so sad. Once inside the facility what caught my attention was a large white box in the front of the room. My neighbor appeared to be sleeping in the box and I wondered why no one was *waking* her up. The next thing I knew everyone was lining up for her viewing. Feeling something awful was about to happen I became frightened and tried to pull away from mom. Too late, she had a vise grip on my arm dragging me the whole way. When we arrived at the foot of the box I closed my eyes while mom led me along. Suddenly stopping, I thought we were past the box and I felt it was safe to open my eyes. There I was face to face with my sleeping neighbor. Sensing I was about to have a meltdown mom hastily snatched me away to find our seats. The services started but at no time did anyone attempt to wake my friend. I just knew the loud singing would be the very thing to do that. But no, she slept right through the entire thing. I never did find out why it was called a *wake* since no one ever woke up.

This experience was terrifying and for a long time afterward I refused to be alone in the bathroom. A similar looking white box was in there – the bathtub. My older sister was the only one who understood my plight and went with me when I needed to use bathroom and slept with me knowing I was having nightmares. Having her close was my only comfort. It took a long time for me to understand the finality of death. For many years I refused to attend any funeral.

When I was nine, my sister left home to start her own family. My plea to go with her was denied. My playmate, teacher and best friend was suddenly missing from my world. This was the first time I experienced a deep sense of loss, sadness and depression. My younger siblings couldn't fill the emptiness in my heart. As far as I was concerned, the babies were just little noise makers sleeping most of the time or needed diaper changes, no fun at all.

SUMMER IN THE WOODS

A couple of years after my sister left home, our family had grown by two more children. Needing a larger home the decision was made to relocate to Chicago, Illinois. Since dad's job was in Chicago, he would remain there while our new house was being built. In the meantime the rest of us packed up and moved to a furnished rental log cabin in a wooded area of Wisconsin. Our TV was packed in storage with other household furniture so mom showed us another form of entertainment, discovering other life found in the woods all around us.

That summer had endless days of warm sunshine filtering through the trees. Birds softly chirping woke us early, and laughter of children filled the cabin. Fun was an everyday activity. Hiking through the woods surrounding the property was enjoyable as well as educational. While exploring mom taught us the names of several woodland creatures spotted in the area; foxes, bobcats and the occasional deer roaming throughout the property. Spiders, bugs and other creepy things also called the woods home. Mom showed us eggs from a fallen bird's nest and animal tracks that led to their hiding places. Families of beavers were busy building a dam while ducks swam noisily in the millpond. Wild rabbits hopped in and out of view while squirrels scurried up and down trees storing nuts for the winter. I taught my brothers how to safely climb trees and walk the length of fallen logs lying on the ground.

Wild flowers grew everywhere. Daily we brought mom fresh bouquets to place on our dinner table. Sometimes the flowers turned out to be pretty weeds, she knew the difference, we never did. Out exploring one day we found patches of strawberries and grapes growing in the wild. After stuffing our faces with as much as we could eat, we ran home to show mom what we found. Giving us empty grocery bags she sent us out to gather as much as we could carry. While we were gone, mom was busy baking her lighter than air homemade bread. The aroma of bread baking drifting through the woods brought us running home. Imagine our delight when she turned those batches of strawberries and grapes into delicious jelly. With apple trees nearby, we were sent to gather ones fallen on the ground. These were turned into apple sauce and fried apple rings for our pancakes. Mom created a lot of magic in the kitchen.

Dad came to visit every other weekend with an extended stay during summer holidays. We always had a grand time when he was with us. Each visit we were surprised with special treats, huge watermelons, sacks of oranges and bags of nuts or new toys to play with. Every visit brought details of progress on the new house. One weekend he took us to Chicago to see the progress for ourselves. Only half way finished he explained it wouldn't be long before completion. None the less we were excited to see the new neighborhood and a glimpse of future friends. A couple of days later we were on the road heading back to the cabin. We then started to count down the days to leaving for the city. Arriving back at the cabin dad took the time to improve conditions for us kids. One day he took a length of rope tying one end to a sturdy tree branch and the other end to a large tractor tire creating a swing. Another time he bought a wading pool for us to cool off in during the long hot summer days. Several times he took us to a nearby lake and taught us to skip rocks across the water and helped us collect sea shells scattered along the shore. Weekends ended way too soon and he had to leave getting back to work. Huddling together he hugged us, dried a few tears and promised to be back as soon as he could. Mom knew we were sad to see him leave. As soon as he was on the road she walked us down the sandy back road to the country store for ice cream cones. The ice cream eased the absence of dad but only for a while.

The day after Labor Day meant it was time to start the new school year. Fondly, we referred to school as the brain factory. I was amazed to see how small the country school was. There were three grade levels in each classroom. Teachers, all 3 of them, taught lessons according to grade level ability. This school structure was different, far more laid back than my previous school. Many afternoon recesses were extended if a softball game was still going on, and classroom studies didn't seem to be a priority.

A noticeable chill in the air was a clear indication the fall season was upon us. Trees were carpeting the ground with multicolored leaves, and flocks of geese noisily honking over head flying in their signature V formation heading south further announced the changing season. The cabin hadn't been insulated and the chill outside was coming through the walls. The wood burning stove provided minimal warmth so mom piled all the blankets on the largest bed and we all sleep together. Summer of 1962 had been a magical time. Sadly it would be the last time we would be happy together as a family.

Two weeks before Thanksgiving we left Wisconsin to move into our new home. Dad had already moved in our furniture from storage. The new house was much larger than our previous home in Indiana but, then again, so was our family. Sadly, the love, peace and happiness we shared beforehand did not follow us. Children can sense discord between their parents, we knew something was wrong. Dad worked long hours and mom was sad most of the time, no more laughter, hugs or spontaneous kisses from her. Mom's anguish affected us as well. We were in mourning for the loss of the mom we knew. The saddest part was the inability to make her happy again. Within a year, our parents separated and eventually divorced. Their ending was distressing and each of us suffered in our own way. As a pre-teen with my older sister and now mom gone, my childhood was cut short. I was suddenly thrust into the adult world of responsibility.

Dad was our custodial parent, and I became a parent figure to my younger siblings. Even at this young age, I was aware that for the family to survive, a great deal of mom's job would rest on my shoulders. Knowing if dad was also gone, we would be in real trouble. With that in mind, I stepped up to the plate and took on the obligation to help keep what was left of our family together.

Dad taught vehicle mechanic repair at a local high school. With so many mouths to feed he also worked on the weekends as a flight instructor teaching students to fly airplanes. Sometimes he would take us flying with him, but after he did the barrel rolls we were too terrified to go up again. The puddle on the ground that previously had been breakfast convinced him of that. Consequently, none of us stayed with flying long enough to earn a pilot's license.

With dad working so much, I was tagged as "it" to take care of the home. He left for work at 6:30 a.m. leaving me with the responsibility to prepare breakfast and get us off to school. About this time, I learned to use mom's sewing machine to make and repair clothes, mend ripped sheets, do laundry, help with homework, and cook our meals. This was quite a task for someone not yet a teenager, but that was life as I knew it. My siblings resented me being in charge and telling them what to do. I wasn't mom, so the resentment was understandable. The refusal to follow my "orders" to get their homework and chores done generally resulted in arguments with occasional fights. They were on the offense, and I was on the defense. Frequently this drama resulted in butt tearing when dad came home tired from work and walked in on chaos. Being responsible for younger siblings was in many ways like permanently living in a carnival crazy house while being in the middle of a never ending nightmare. In their minds if I wasn't there mom could come back home. They alternated between resenting me and blaming me for mom being gone. On the other hand they appreciated me for being the safeguard keeping us from being split up and going to foster care. This frightened each of us. Foster care meant we would lose touch with mom. For us, this was not a viable option. Eventually my siblings figured out that if they did what they were supposed to do, the problem would be solved.

This responsibility taught me useful negotiation skills. Not cooking meals until the work was done worked like a charm. Reflecting on those days, I realize I was being prepared for my future military career and life in general. Being told numerous times in my life, "God prepares you for every mission He has for you, if He leads you to it, He will see you through it". My life story gives testament to this as an accurate statement.

After the divorce, mom was no longer in our home but she was always involved in our lives. She loved us, but she had [at the time] five undiagnosed brain tumors. This condition caused her to be unable to work full time or take care of us on her own. CAT [Computerized Axial Tomography] scans were not yet available so one knew how much pain she suffered her entire life. A year before her passing she was finally diagnosed with these tumors. Her doctors indicated she was born with these benign abnormalities that grew slowly over her life time. This explained her debilitating headaches.

Children growing up without their mother miss out on many things. We lack a mother's love providing encouragement along the way, no one to confide in, or dry tears when hurt. Mother's Day opens wounds that bring fresh pain and tears to a child's spirit. Others do their best to fill the emptiness, but the absence of mom is always felt. There is no greater love than that of a mother, and no greater hurt when she isn't there. Mom encouraged us with her undying love and always showed up just when we needed her. Our mom passed away several decades ago, her love, words of wisdom, and encouragement resonate in our lives even to this day.

When I started high school dad enrolled me in home economic classes, cooking and sewing. The first Thanksgiving turkey I prepared was a disaster. Doing what I thought I saw mom do didn't turn out well at all. I failed to properly stuff the turkey. When I removed the top of the roaster I was devastated to see the turkey caved in and swimming in its juices. I woke dad to show him the mess. He fell out laughing saying the bird looked like it was doing the back stroke in the roasting pan. Seeing my disappointment, he took me to the grocery store to buy another bird. When we returned home dad called his sister to provide instructions on how to "properly" stuff the bird. The second time around the turkey came out much better. Learning to prepare more than hot dogs with pork and beans greatly improved the quality and variety of our meals. Sewing enabled me to make dresses and other clothing for my sister and me. Both programs were a win/win for our family.

As my siblings and I grew older, life fell into a comfortable routine. Each of us learned many useful life skills from dad. The boys were taught to repair vehicles from the tires up, my sister and I had the indoor chores. We all helped dad renovate our basement and make repairs around the house and yard. As a young teen, I mastered using all kinds of hand as well as power tools.

I was fourteen years old when dad insisted I learn to drive. Calmly explaining he had to work long hours and needed me to drive taking care of chores in his absence. The station wagon seemed huge, it may as well have been an 18 wheeler truck. Barely being able to see over the steering wheel, learning to drive this vehicle terrified me. The problem was solved by having me sit on two bed pillows providing the needed height to see the road. That worked out just fine. In our alley we set up several metal trash cans spaced a car length apart so I could practice my parallel parking. Jokingly, our neighbors watched and took bets as to how many cans I would hit each time. There were many trash can casualties but I eventually mastered this task as well. The fact that I didn't have a driver's license or even a learner's permit didn't seem to worry dad at all. His only advice to me was to "be careful." And so I was.

Always trying to hold things together, I did what I remembered watching mom do. One winter everyone came down with nasty colds. Without cold medication in the house, I decided to make hot toddies the way she made them. I found the tea bags, honey, lemon juice and rum dad hid in his closet. I made a pot of tea and put the concoction together. Not knowing the exact measurements I over did it with the rum. As a result, we were all drunk but slept soundly that night. The good news is the colds were gone, the bad news is we had wicked hangovers.

At some point the authorities discovered we were often home alone. Dad and I were summoned to court to justify our family situation. The judge listened attentively to our story but indicated I was far too young to have that level of responsibility. I replied to him that I had been taking care of us for several years. He looked at me in absolute astonishment. Taking this into consideration his temporary judgment was to have court ordered, unannounced home visits to evaluate our circumstances. Dad and I would return to court for the judge to make his final ruling.

Returning home that day dad was exhausted. Worry and concern was etched deeply on his face. He immediately went to bed for much needed rest. I gathered my siblings for a family meeting to explain what happened at court. Emphasizing that a negative report to the judge would cause us to be split up and sent to other families somewhere in China. We had to keep the house clean and no arguing or fighting. Bluffing them was a reliable way to get them to behave. Mastering this "mind control" technique over them proved beneficial from then on.

For the next six months there was peace and harmony at home. No arguing, fighting or misbehaving by anyone. The court sent the visitors at random. We never saw the same lady twice. Each one seemed to be cut from the same stern cookie cutter. Their no nonsense demeanor reminded me of the wicked witch of the West and the truant officers schools sent to a child's home when someone skipped school.

The visits could take place on a Sunday morning at 7:15, a Tuesday at 10 o'clock at night, or any given Thursday at 5:00 in the afternoon. Sometimes there would be three visits a week and every once in a blue moon, they would skip a week. Each visit included a walk through the entire house room by room. During these visits, I was quizzed about how I ran the household, the meals I made, and how often clothes got washed, etc. Many times I was given useful tips on how to do something that would make my life easier. Pine cleaner used as a pre-soak took stains out of cloths and baking soda added to the wash freshen the load. If out of furniture polish a dab of mayonnaise on a clean dust rag would clean the wood leaving a nice shine

My two youngest brothers were always frightened when these visits occurred. They asked me why we couldn't just run away and hide out with our older sister in Wisconsin. I responded with the fact that we didn't have any food or money, and it was too far to walk. They didn't like my answer but eventually accepted it.

Always thinking ahead, the idea to run away had the wheels spinning in my mind to put a contingency plan in motion. I was already driving, so that piece was covered. I was sure dad would not give us gas and food money or the use of his car to run away. Then it dawned on me, I controlled the weekly food money. Since I did the grocery shopping anyway, I started buying only sale items. It took a while saving the change, eventually I accumulated about $35. I kept this stash hidden away. I knew dad kept a map in his car, so I pulled it out and studied the route to Wisconsin. With my preparation finished, all I had to do was wait to see what the final decision from the court would be. I knew better than to share this information with the others, they were little blabber mouths that would foil my plan.

Miraculously, the kids behaved during our probation period. We made sure there was never an incident to report. Finally, six months later, we went back to court. The judge took his sweet time reading through the document set before him. He read for a minute or so, peered over his glasses and looked at either my dad or at me, read a little further, and finally he addressed us. He stated that each of the social workers had nothing but praise for how well our family functioned. His ruling was final, we would remain together as a family. A wave of relief washed over me knowing I wouldn't need to put my alternative plan into action.

The six months of peace and tranquility were over. Foolishly, at dinner that night dad announced the probation period was over and we would remain together as a family. Now tell me **WHY** he had to go and do that. Unknowingly he had given them permission to go back to turmoil. None the less, we survived it all and lived to tell the tale together. As we got older, life got better as we learned to rely on each other. Each of us became independent and responsible at a very young age. This experience proved to be a valuable lesson serving me well for the rest of my life.

At some point during this unsettling time I turned to our large family Bible. I read seeking help for my family. Somewhere within the pages there had to be answers. From *Genesis* to *Revelations,* I read many stories of how God performed miracles and changed lives for the better. Daily I prayed asking Him to fix our family putting us back together again. We missed and needed our mom. At this point only God could fix this situation. Some nights I scanned the skies searching for angels to rescue us. Liberation never came, so for a while I lost faith. With my life so hectic I didn't dwell on it for long. During my darkest hours, feeling at the end of all hope, I felt a calming but unseen protecting force all around me. Maybe angels were there after all watching over each of us.

Completing high school I went to college and earned my degree. By this time I was tired of school and yearned for something more exciting to do. I was weary of life with family and needed a break. I wanted to travel beyond my hometown and see what the rest of the world was like. While watching TV one night, an Army commercial came on. Apparently they had 444 jobs available, I decided one of them had my name on it.

LESSONS LEARNED FROM MILITARY LIFE

My introduction to the military began with basic training at Fort McClellan, Alabama. Unlike most females in my platoon, males did not intimidate me in the least. Drill sergeants by design put "the fear of God" in trainees while teaching military procedures. Their no nonsense demeanor could be quite intimidating. Living in Chicago and life with my siblings eliminated fear of this kind all together. If it came down to it, I knew I could take them on and win. Being from Chicago had another advantage. When word got around where I was from, my platoon nicknamed me "Mafia Anne". I suppose Chicago's past history of notorious gangsters set the tone for that. At any rate, having this nick name gave me a bit of status implying that I was someone not to "mess with". Worked for me.

Basic training for me was more like a paid vacation. No one to look after, cook for, or argue with. Life was my own for the very first time. I was responsible only for myself. Military discipline was right up my alley. I developed an appreciation for a code of conduct, procedures, protocol, and having a measurable set of expectations to gauge my progress. I realized it was possible to push past fatigue, doubts, and fear. Low - crawling through mud under concertina wire at night with machine guns on full automatic blaring overhead and throwing a live hand grenade can be a very frightening experience. I learned there are many things in life that are fear based. The solution to survival is to push past the fear and kept going.

Drill and Ceremony [D & C] teaches various movements and commands. Drill sergeants spent entire days teaching us to march in formation, rank recognition, when and whom to salute, facing movements, general orders, and other aspects of the military. It may sound strange, but for me, this was fun, reminding me of my early childhood playing with friends. Whenever we had down time several of us in my platoon practiced D & C as entertainment. Learning these procedures so well, our drill sergeant would occasionally utilize us as demonstrators assisting others. Another favorite activity was calling cadence while marching or on a platoon run. We made up a few cadences that we only sang while cleaning the barracks.

One part of Army life I needed to adjust to was waking up long before the sun was up. This is known as O'dark thirty hours. Being awake at 4:00 a.m., with sleep still in our eyes doing our details prior to breakfast at 5:00 a.m. became a way of life. Little did I know that all this training would be put to good use several years down the road.

After graduating from basic training, my next assignment sent me to Fort Lee, Virginia for Advance Individual Training [AIT]. This proved to be even more fun than basic training. After morning classes we had loads of free time to do what we wanted. Not a drill sergeant in sight. My job training was in logistics. In Army terms, this was called your MOS or Military Occupation Specialty. Having my college degree earned me the rank of PFC [private first class]. Being the senior ranking private in my platoon our sergeant made me her assistant, the platoon guide. I had 118 females I was responsible for. Our barracks was an open bay separated by partitions into four person cubicles. That summer was terribly hot, and the huge fan in the barracks barely cooled things down. It was too hot to sleep, and 04:00 hours rolled around just as we could drift off during the coolest hours of the morning. The soldier on CQ [charge of quarters] woke us via the intercom long before the chirping of birds did.

Being in charge of the platoon was no big deal, raising my sister and brothers taught me how to take charge, solve problems quickly and efficiently get the job done. The platoon and I worked as a well oiled machine. Together we kept the floor in our barracks polished to a mirror shine and personal areas were at all times inspection ready. Helping each other with details and classroom studies resembled a school setting more so than a military barracks. I kept problems within the platoon counseling soldiers myself rather than passing the situation up the chain of command. Some of my ladies were homesick, missed their husbands or children and wanted to go AWOL [absent without leave]. To prevent that from happening I procured extra telephone privileges for them. Over time, everyone in the chain of command took note of my leadership ability. As a reward for making my platoon sergeant look good with zero failed barracks inspections and no AWOLs, she put me in for an Army Commendation Metal [ARCOM]. Receiving that award right out of AIT was a big deal. I didn't comprehend the enormity of it at the time, but it played a significant role when I applied to Officer Candidate School [OCS] a few years later. Prior to graduating my new orders reassigned me to Germany.

Arriving in Germany I was assigned to a headquarters unit in Darmstadt. As an enlisted soldier, I lived in the barracks sharing a four person room. The four of us always looked out for each other. We were enjoying life overseas having the opportunity to experience living in another country. I loved everything about Germany, the food, people, and the picturesque old world charm of the countryside. We often went to the wine tasting festivals, sampled the various kinds of sausages, and roamed the outdoor markets. Meeting many Germans I learned a great deal about their country that had strikingly differences from my own. For one, their grade school children attended classes for a half day on Saturday. Germany also had far more holidays than we do. The German highway [the autobahn] didn't have a speed limit, the exception was while driving through a construction zone. By now with all my siblings grown and out living their own lives, dad had the house to himself. He enjoyed the tasty treats I regularly sent home. The Eiswein and various types of smoked sausages and cheeses were his favorites. We often talked about him coming to Germany for a visit, he did, but not until several years later.

As with every place I was stationed, guys tried me either by intimidation of their senior rank or outright lying. The first time any one of them got out of line, my "Chicago mouth" put that person in check ending the confrontation. That happened a few times. It's what we females referred to as "jacking up" a dude. These incidents got around the barracks faster than texting does today. Even though a good number of guys were wonderful friends that females could trust and always count on, there was an abundance of "dirt bags," "morons," and "dip sticks" needing to be "jacked up." There were plenty of them. I remember overhearing a senior Non Commissioned Officer (NCO) telling someone I never needed to carry a weapon since my mouth was fully locked and loaded on automatic fire. I don't quite remember it that way, but it is what it is.

My first job was in the motor pool making sure that each of the unit's vehicles were scheduled for maintenance service when needed and ordering parts for repairs. Here I learned the importance of taking care of my own vehicle. A year later I was transferred to the aviation section where I fell in love with the Bell UH-1 Iroquois [Huey], and the OH-58 Kiowa helicopters. During slow days the pilots would let any of us enlisted personnel tag along on maintenance or check flights. As the supply specialist I ordered repair parts for each of the aircrafts. The enlisted males were crew chiefs, the mechanics for the helicopters. During down time, they taught me how to crew the aircrafts. However, the section OIC [Officer In Charge] refused to let me add this skill as a secondary MOS.

The next three years of enlisted life further honed my discipline and leadership skills. I learned that every task at hand had to be completed right then and there because many more tasks were right behind them. Along the way I learned it was OK to once in a while drop a rubber ball, but never a glass ball. In time I learned the difference between the two.

Nearing the end of my first overseas tour, several senior NCOs and a couple of officers advised me to apply for Officer Candidate

School. Letters of recommendation were written and placed in my personnel folder. About this same time I was promoted to specialist 5 [spec 5], rank equivalent to Sergeant. I was now officially an NCO. A few months later Permanent Change of Station (PCS) orders were cut assigning me to Fort Belvoir, Virginia.

The high point of that assignment was volunteering for the honor detail. The daily detail, retreat, was lowering the flag at precisely 17:00 hours [5 p.m.] each day. When the first note of retreat sounded, every soldier in or out of uniform stopped and saluted the flag. Once the flag was lowered, our detail carefully folded the flag returning it to it's case. The respect and reverence for the American flag has left a lasting impression on me.

Another duty was performing military funerals. In those days a bugler accompanied the detail to play taps during the ceremony. We wore the class A dress uniform with the pant legs bloused into our boots. Our white pistol belts with a black helmet liner for head gear completed the uniform. We were each given three rounds of live ammunition for our M-16 rifles. The detail is aware that the mourning family and friends of the deceased may be wary of our weapons. Being mindful of this, we always kept our detail a respectable distance from the ceremony. With taps completed, after firing our weapons we marched to the flag draped coffin and silently fold the flag. As the team leader it was my duty [and honor] to present the flag to the designated family member. At every funeral our team officiated for, we each felt honored to be a part of our fallen comrade's final ceremony. I'll never forget the experience. Fort Belvoir would be my last assignment as an enlisted soldier. I applied to and was accepted into the OCS program. Orders were cut and I was off to Fort Benning, Georgia.

By this time I was well seasoned in military life. However, this next stage of training was far more challenging than the previous four years. Training at this level is designed to test endurance, develop leadership skills, and hone confidence in one's abilities to make and execute command decisions. Equally important was having integrity above reproach.

Many times our integrity was tested. If any of us knew another soldier was cheating, lying, or misbehaving in any way unbecoming an officer, we were obligated to inform the cadre. On more than a few occasions, members of the cadre sat in the parking lot at night watching the pizza man delivering stacks of pizzas to our barracks. In a civilian situation this would be a normal occurrence, however during this phase of training pizzas were strictly off limits as were all snack and soda vending machines in the barrack's day room. Junk food is referred to as "contraband items". Just after the pizzas were delivered, as the soldiers were passing slices around, several tactical officers came in and confiscated the booty. Anyone caught denying involvement in any of the pizza capers were put out of the program under the integrity violation. A career ender.

After spending time as an enlisted soldier, OCS wasn't a total shock, just more intense. We thought of this experience as basic training on steroids. We spent weeks in concentrated training and studying Army manuals. During phase 1 we weren't allowed to walk anywhere, it was double time, running everywhere we went. Meals were eaten in less than three minutes. From the first in to the last out, the entire company passed through the mess hall in 18 minutes flat and back outside in a company formation. During that phase, I have no idea what I ate. I just inhaled what was on my plate and hit the exit. Phases 2 and 3 were a little more relaxed but still challenging. A couple of times I remember being so tired that I just wanted to quit. Many of us felt this way at different times. From wake-up call to lights out, every minute of our days were filled with activity. Everything from the obstacle and confidence courses, learning the function and use of various weapons to map reading and land navigation created long tiring days. My roommate and several close friends helped me keep it together. We all had to suck it up and drive on knowing each day brought us closer to graduation. Staying focused to keep going and remembering our motto, "for this too shall pass" got us through another day. In the mail one day I received a post card from my favorite aunt. The picture was of an orange and white kitten barely hanging from a tiny tree limb. The caption read "hang in there." And so I did.

My most difficult time was during the last week of training - Range Week. We spent the entire week in the field constantly on the move. We carried fully loaded duffle bags on our backs, carrying our M16 rifle at port arms, sleeping in fox holes, and eating MREs [meals ready to eat]. Marching down a sandy back road in the Georgia heat was trying. Being continuously on the move pushed us to the brink of near exhaustion. The last leg of this exercise was a ten mile forced road march back to garrison. We were told this entire exercise was designed to build our stamina and help further develop our character proving to us we could accomplish far more than we thought we could. The cadre didn't mention we would have calluses on our hands and feet, smell like a herd of wild goats rolling around in a pig sty. They also didn't mention the ten pounds of weight we would each lose while on this field trip. That part wasn't necessarily a bad thing.

Our platoon made a pledge that no one would quit and get on the straggler's truck. The vehicle was provided for soldiers that for whatever reason could not go any further on the march. At one point, due to heat exhaustion, I started to drift back from my platoon. Two of my closest male friends saw this and drifted back to where I was and poured their canteens of cold water over me helping me to revive. They both had been with cadre on the recon [reconnaissance] for this march and knew the route. They assured me we were within a quarter mile of the barracks, and this road march ended Range Week. Once we rounded that last bend, lo and behold, there dead ahead were the barracks rising like a mirage. Home at last.

After cleaning and stowing our equipment, we showered and changed into civilian clothes. The dinner meal was a special treat, a picnic style steak dinner with all the fixings. The dozen or so that rode the stragglers vehicle were not allowed to partake of this meal. They ate whatever the mess hall had prepared for them, probably more MREs. Being more exhausted than hungry, I chose to skip the meal and chose to sit on the shower room floor letting the warm water cascade over me. Knowing where I was, my roommate brought me a plate of food. God bless her.

In due time graduation day came. We were excited, yet somewhat apprehensive about our future assignments. A senior officer spoke to our graduating class assuring us that all the tough times we suffered was in preparation for our careers as officers. Wherever our assignments took us, we would look back with understanding and appreciation for this experience. A new set of challenges were about to emerge. Each of us were given our reassignment orders and wished well with our careers. A final salute and we were dismissed. As a newly minted 2nd lieutenant, I was off to Fort Dix, New Jersey.

Thinking on my feet and making decisions affecting soldiers became a way of life. "Just make it happen" and "do more with less" became the catch phrase of the military. Each promotion brought more challenging assignments balanced with learned experience to draw from. Being able to quickly adapt to changing circumstances is something I mastered a long time ago.

My favorite assignment will always be my command in Bad Kreuznach, Germany. My boss, a full colonel, supported everything I did in my company, and I supported my soldiers with everything they needed for their careers, education, and families. Always marching to a different drummer, I decided to change the rules in the barracks where most of my enlisted soldiers lived. Having experienced barracks life as enlisted, I knew how dreary and mundane it was to have each room a carbon copy of every other room. I allowed my soldiers to set their rooms up with personal touches of their choosing. I did away with the military olive drab blankets and allowed civilian bedding. During random room inspections, the soldier's rooms were a delight to see. Each room looked like a cross between a college dormitory room and a military barracks. My soldiers loved this freedom to express themselves in this manner. Troop morale was at an all time high. My only concern was having approval of the colonel. Early in my career I learned it is easier to seek forgiveness than ask for permission. After the barrack rooms were painted and set up, I had the colonel scheduled to do a pay day, class A uniform and barracks inspection. The colonel was military to the core, and I had no idea how he would react to these changes. I never let a shred of fear show, or as another soldier put it "never let them see you sweat". To my surprise and delight, the colonel loved it. Explaining to him that this is where these soldiers lived is all that was necessary to say. I had his one hundred percent approval.

For the first year and a half of my command I never had to administer any Uniform Code of Military Justice (UCMJ) disciplinary actions, also known as an article 15. That changed after Desert Storm/Desert Shield developed. A few soldiers thought if they become a problem it would be grounds for a discharge from the Army. Bad call, stop/loss kept everyone right where they were. Eventually, life settled back down, and it was time to change command. Orders were cut reassigning me stateside. After living in Germany for over nine years, it was heart breaking to leave this wonderful country. Nevertheless, orders were cut sending me to Fort Benjamin Harrison, Indiana. This assignment was as an instructor teaching 2nd lieutenants military logistics and maintenance courses. Considered an easy assignment, everyone in my section had time to finish our civilian education earning Master's degrees.

Ultimately my military career came to an end. Transitioning to civilian life was challenging. I asked where the latrine was instead of the ladies' room, I used military time as a substitute for civilian time. Converting military job experience to civilian employment was almost impossible to translate. Not finding anything suitable, as a last resort I decided to use my military education benefits to complete a second BS degree in law enforcement. Even with that degree, no civilian job materialized. Either I was over qualified, under qualified, lacked experience or a hiring freeze was in effect. Additional school seemed like a good idea, so I tried my hand at law school. I did a year but never grasped the concept of how the law works from a legal standpoint. To me, either something is right or wrong with limiting shades of gray. Either someone did the crime or they didn't.

With time on my hands, I decided to do volunteer work with my church preparing meals for the homeless. I found this work to be very satisfying. Experiencing a side of society I had never before witnessed firsthand was an eye opener. Learning individual stories showed me just how life can be changed in an instant. The loss of a job or a serious illness can create a domino effect leading to isolation and/or depression. In desperation a few turned to drugs to escape the reality of their life. Others lost family and found themselves living on the streets. A small number were in transition to another job. It was heart breaking to see so many people in need of everything I took for granted. This experience taught me to be more sympathetic and understanding opening my eyes to be more aware of those less fortunate. It cost nothing to open your heart to help another. I enjoyed this work, but after a couple of years God made it clear He had other plans in mind for me. I was about to begin a new chapter of life.

A NEW JOURNEY BEGINS

A phone call with a simple request from some relatives took my life down an unforeseen detour. I was asked to come and get their children giving them time to get their lives back on track. The kids were very young, several were still in Pampers. I reminded them I had a small house and to get a move on with getting their lives in order. Nonetheless, I had a funny feeling the situation with the children would last a lot longer than expected. Time would prove me right.

Our family has always protected and helped each other through tough times. Surviving much worse, I agreed to be there by the weekend. It was a long drive from Indiana to get the children, so I chose to spend the time in prayer communicating with God. I told Him I had no idea of how I could support all these little kids. Imploring His help, I asked for clear guidance. While driving I felt His presence all around me. A familiar calmness enveloped me as I opened my soul to His presence of pure unconditional love.

One of mom's sisters, my favorite aunt, had taken me under her wing teaching me to trust that unseen guiding presence available to each soul. As little kids all of us, cousins and siblings alike, were afraid of her. Insisting on obedience and honesty to us she was mean and scary. She would make us sit at the dinner table and eat those dreadful vegetables and everything else on our plates. Her eyes were the most frightening thing about her. She had soft brown eyes, but when questioning you about something, those eyes were unsettling. It literally felt as if she had laser beam power to penetrate my skull invading every thought in my mind. In no time, without her ever saying a word, she had me telling everything on myself and spilling the beans on everyone else as well. When I was a teenager my aunt moved to the east coast to complete her Master's degree in special education.

Several years later while stationed at Fort Belvoir, Virginia she and I became very close. She taught me how to walk with God, firmly placing my hand in His. There were never a series of lectures but rather leading by example. While watching the news one night, a brutal murder was reported. My response was to let the creep burn in hell. Her response was to ask God to forgive the man and pray for his soul. She calmly explained the murderer was clearly in emotional and spiritual pain needing God's love, not condemnation. This was a new concept for me. I had always assumed these were just mean people. It never occurred to me someone may commit crimes due to internal pain. Lashing out at others was how they found a way to release pent up frustration, anger and hurt. Her explanation opened my heart. Compassion was further explained on another occasion. While waking from a deep sleep one morning I clearly heard a message in my mind I felt came from God, "if you deny a blessing to anyone, you have also denied a blessing to yourself". I called my aunt for clarification. She validated the message did indeed originate from a higher plane and further emphasized its meaning adding "*you always reap what you sow*", if you harbor negative thoughts or feelings toward any one, you attract negative conditions into your own life. Her spiritual insight was very deep. For many years she planted spiritual seeds in my heart.

Without being conscientiously aware of it, she was peeling back layer upon layer of hurt, anger, and mistrust from my soul. Gradually the all embracing healing light of God's love permeated to my soul. I was beginning to understand what she meant about patience being a natural state of being for those that trust the Lord. The most crucial message she relayed was "when God ask you to do something He has the means to do it already planned out". Asking her how someone would know it is actually God asking, she looked me straight in the eye and calmly said, "something in your heart will stir, and you will know". Spending time with her had been a spiritual transformation. The seeds of wisdom she planted took root and continue to grow.

My aunt was very important to me. When she left this world in 1994 I was devastated. Having been sick for the previous year, our daily visits were via phone calls. The day before she passed, she asked me not to call the next day, instead she would call me. That call never came. Early the next morning her husband called stating she had slipped into a coma. Knowing she wouldn't last much longer he asked me to come as quickly as I could. I packed a bag and rushed to the airport. After checking in, I realized my flight wouldn't leave for another hour and a half.

Finding my departure gate completely vacant, I decided to watch the airplanes landing and taking off. At precisely 11 a.m. I felt the warm energy of her soul pass right through me. At that moment I knew she had departed this life. Grateful for the solitude, I let salty tears roll unchecked down my face. Even though I was in my forties I felt like an abandoned child. Life was drained from me,

I was completely numb. She was gone and so was my reason for living.

As only God can do it, comfort came in the form of a senior member of my church. The pastor was on my flight headed to a conference on the east coast. Seeing me in a state of grief, he sensed something was terribly wrong. Explaining what happened he held my hands leading a prayer right there in the airport terminal. My cousins met me when we landed, the expression on their faces confirmed what I already knew. She was gone. Seeing our anguish the pastor gathered us together and led a prayer for our aunt and for us to find a measure of peace in her passing. Thanking him we left the airport. Instead of going to the house, we went to the funeral home to see if we could spend just a few minutes with her. By the time we got there, the facility had already closed.

Early the next morning we went back to the funeral home. The staff allowed us to sit with her for a few minutes. She looked as if she were peacefully sleeping. I asked for and was given a pair of scissors. Cutting a long piece of my hair I carefully placed it in her hand to be cremated with her. As I gently kissed her goodbye I promised to live a good life so I could see her again in heaven.

The sadness I initially felt quickly spiraled into a tsunami of grief. The bottomless pit of depression held me like quicksand. My soul was screaming out to God for understanding as to why He took her from me. My heart was shattered into a million pieces. My guiding light was snuffed out, and I was adrift on a sea of despair.

Returning home from the funeral, I developed a migraine and slept for three days. Somehow, and I can't readily explain it, while sleeping my soul was put on a type of spiritual life support. I was aware the layers of anguish, grief and pain were being peeled away allowing the calming warmth of God's love to flow through me once more.

Once I could think clearly I went to see my pastor. I felt certain there was absolutely no reason for me being alive with my aunt gone. Understanding my grief he assured me that God called my aunt home because it was her time to go. He would call me home when it was my time. I am alive because God has further work for me. When the situation with the children came about I knew he was right. I needed to be here for them.

With memories of my aunt and her lessons in mind, I set aside all doubt and fear. Forgeing ahead I put my faith in action knowing I wasn't alone on this mission. She taught me God will do much more than I could ever dream. When it comes to blessings you just can't outdo God. He will lead you through the darkest valley and the loneliest wilderness providing everything needed each step of the way. As Moses trusted God to part the Red Sea, He whispered to my heart "stand back and see what I will do". Little did I know the adventure with the children would be an unforgettable experience.

It was the middle of winter and snow was getting deeper the further north I drove. Snow along my route almost reached the top of the tires of my van. Coming off the highway, I was appreciative of the previous drivers that left tracks for me to follow. When dad saw me arrive a wave of relief fell across his face. His expression relayed gratitude for the Calvary arriving to liberate his house. Sheer joy radiated from his face. As I walked into his house, kids were ripping and running all over the place. The number of children would form a small platoon.

Absolute panic washed over me. Once again I wondered what the hell was I doing. I started to question the sanity of agreeing to do this. Dad gave me $20 to stop at a fast food restaurant to feed the kids on the way home. Before we could leave the youngest children needed a pamper change. With that done it was time to hit the road. We packed up their things, loaded up the van, kissed everyone goodbye, and off we went. I will never forget the big smile on dad's face as he waved good bye.

The chaotic behavior in the van on the way home was a preview of coming events. They fought over toys, threw toys at each other, unbuckled seat belts, rolled over the seat to the back row and on and on. While driving my mind was flashing back to this same drama with my siblings. This time around military basic training techniques would be the best course of action to take. This would work for girls as well as boys. I was in command, and they were soon to be under control. Subconsciously I realized raising these children was the request God would have me do. Everything I had done in my life led to this moment, failure was not a viable option. And so it began.

Arriving home fighting over toys continued. Toys aimed for someone else hit me and my dogs. The kids were running around completely out of control. My previously peaceful home had become a combat zone. That first night was a nightmare. Getting the children to settle down resembled a circus ring master corralling the large wild cats into their proper positions. Apparently, the kids had a mission of their own, to seek and destroy everything in their paths. The huge tub of toys they brought were weapons of mass destruction. Getting them fed, a bath, Pamper changes, into pajamas and off to bed was a time consuming ordeal. I would get them in bed, turn off the light and leave the room. Before I could walk down the hall, a couple of them would be up playing with things in the bedroom. The older children wanted to stay up all night watching TV, and no one was used to doing chores. As I lay in bed that night, actually I was on the couch, I wondered just what the hell I had gotten myself into this time. I remembered having that same thought my first night at basic training and then again my first night at OCS. Well, I survived those incidents and with God's help, I knew I would survive this as well.

A couple of days later a convoy of vehicles rolled into my driveway. Several friends from church brought a high chair, booster seats, clothes, food, toys, and various other items needed for the children. To say this was a blessing would be an understatement. There were enough supplies to tide me over until my next payday. As time went on, God sent many organizations, people and families that went out of their way to rally round us. I refer to them collectively as my support battalion.

BASIC TRAINING REPURPOSED

This whole scenario was eerily familiar, was this **déjà vu**? Been there, done that. With all the chaos I felt like I was back at home with my siblings, only this time I was the adult. Well meaning parents advised me to put the kids in "time out" to correct their behavior. Really, time out. Around here that was a joke. Sitting in a corner for ten minutes accomplished nothing. On the other hand, five minutes of standing at parade rest while explaining to me why the offender thought it was a good idea to throw their shoes on the roof of the house or flush a roll of toilet paper down the commode worked wonders.

From day one, I set the behavior standards. The first thing I had to do was teach them to keep their busy little hands off property that did not belong to them. The kids were then introduced to military style drill and ceremony. *Name, explain,* and *demonstrate* is how soldiers are taught military tasks. Knowing this method to be tried and true, I used this to teach the kids basic chores around the house and yard.

The first order of business was to teach commands: preparatory command and commands of execution. The children thought this was a fun Army game taking to it like a duck takes to water. They learned ATTENTION meant to stop what they were doing and put their eyes on me to wait for further instructions because further instructions were definitely coming. Mastering that maneuver, next they learned PARADE–REST. PARADE is the preparatory command and REST is the command of execution. This command has them stand with their feet about 12 inches apart, arms behind their backs with thumbs interlocked. These two commands were used most often. I taught them the proper body positions for all subsequent commands. Other instructions used when necessary were the front leaning rest [a push – up position], recover [back to a standing position], range walk [walking at a fast pace as opposed to running], and calling cadence when we were on a run around the track. GO and NO GO were either a yes to a request or a denial for that request.

Every so often the kids were introduced to other commands, FALL-IN, means to line up in preparation to go somewhere. FALL-OUT was used to let them know they could move around freely, to exit our vehicle or be dismissed after completing another task. AT-EASE means to stand at a relaxed form of parade rest when I talked to them needing their full attention. AS -YOU -WERE meant they could go back to what they were previously doing. Chores were now called a detail, and room inspections occurred daily. Cleaning trash from the yard is known as doing police call. Area beautification was doing yard work. Cleaning the house is having a GI party. Cleaning the bathroom is latrine detail, and doing dishes became kitchen patrol [KP] duty. Everyone had their assigned work to do. Every Sunday the details rotated. Who ever had KP was also the sergeant for the week. When details were finished, the sergeant accompanied me to do the inspections. If any detail was improperly done, the sergeant had to explain to me why that person failed the inspection. This was done to teach each of them to be responsible for their actions by paying close attention to what they were responsible for. Failed inspections resulted in a re-do on Saturday morning. I did this intentionally to interfere with their plans to spend time with friends. I had to be smarter than the kids.

If they were starting to get out of control, they were told I would tighten up their shot group, either you adjust your attitude or I will adjust it for you. Attempting to explain away bad behavior, they soon understood the maximum effect range of their "excuse" was zero meters. In other words, excuses will get you nowhere. If they messed up something, learn from it, suck it up and drive on. Keep going. If contemplating doing something questionable, my rule of thumb was simple, if you would do it with me standing next to you then it was OK, if not, then don't do it at all. I explained doing anything the wrong way never turns out right. It didn't take long for them to understand I do not reward bad behavior. Good behavior was always recognized and appropriately rewarded.

SUPPORT OPERATIONS

I am truly blessed with wonderful neighbors. When I told them I was bringing the children home they went into action rounding up things little kids needed pledging their help in every way they could. There is no way I could have maintained my sanity during those early days without their constant support. Infrequently they were pressed into babysitting duties while I went to discount department stores to purchase items the kids needed. With their assistance several small swimming pools, a trampoline, and a playground set were assembled. Repairs were made when needed. One neighbor knew of a great fishing spot. Several times we took the little ones out for the day to feed the ducks and enjoy nature. For many years she accompanied us to the school band concerts the kids played in.

Living on a meager retirement check was next to impossible. God was way ahead of me with this having prepared the way ahead of time. Prior to the arrival of the children I volunteered at a soup kitchen. The staff was aware of my new situation with several more mouths to feed, and I was authorized to receive food on pantry day. One of the volunteers along with her four daughters supplied food not available from the pantry. They used lots of coupons, took advantage of store sales and the buy-one-get-one-free deals. Synchronizing with me she knew when I was making a provisions run. She would have pantry items and her family's contributions all set up and ready to go when I arrived. I would be in and out in less than ten minutes. Her family always provided birthday presents, Easter baskets, Christmas toys and other gifts for each of us. During the summer they stock piled school supplies for the next school year. This form of support was multiplied many times over from several different families.

For the next six months I was extremely busy. Once again I was up at O' dark thirty hours getting the day started for the children. Cooking their breakfast and getting them ready for the day was challenging. By comparison, six months of OCS Range Week would have been a nice vacation. The older children were in grade school with another child in pre-school creating a juggling act for me. I had to pack up the younger children, drop off, and then retrieve the pre-schooler, timing this all out was critical. While the older children were in school I had to keep the youngest ones engaged in educational activities to keep their minds active and out of trouble. In the meantime I prepared meals, washed clothes, cleaned the house, and did yard work the kids were too young to do.

God always sent the right support at the right time. The saying "it takes a village to raise a child" is true, before long we had our own support village. In every instance when help or assistance was needed, the solution was there. Our pastor assured me early on that God would provide everything we needed. Trust God to be my guiding light was the message he gave me that day. Coming to the house to meet my little band of darlings he understood why it was not a good idea to bring them to church for a while. None of the children could sit still for five minutes. Before he left I was provided with a list of services that would help with clothing and other forms of support I would need.

Once all the children could sit through church services [1 year later], they enjoyed the sermons. Countless blessings came from our church family. Over the years many parishioners donated toys, bags of clothing, and shoes their children or grandchildren had outgrown. Sometimes much needed and deeply appreciated monetary donations arrived in the mail.

Our first Christmas was nothing short of a miracle. On December 1, after buying food and paying bills, I had less than $50.00 left. With that in mind how do I tell my little ones Santa Clause might not come this year? Feeling helpless, I sent a prayer to heaven that in some way all the children would receive something for the holiday. Fast forwarding to December 24, we had not one but two

Christmas trees complete with ornaments. During the previous three weeks, several families, organizations, their school and a Christmas Store provided food, toys, stuffed animals, clothes, shoes and a wide assortment of other gifts. While everyone was in school or with a babysitter, I made the rounds to gather all the items, bring everything home and find hiding places to store it away. On Christmas Eve I had the children take a large bag of oatmeal outside to sprinkle it over the snow. I explained that the more the reindeer had to munch on, the longer Santa would be in the house. With that news they emptied the entire bag. Being kids, they wanted to stay up to sneak a peek at Santa. Attempting to convince them he only came while children were sleeping fell on deaf ears. Reading *The Night before Christmas* and several more Christmas stories did nothing to make them sleepy. Ignoring them I went to bed and set my alarm for midnight. At the appointed hour, I crept from my bed and listened for sounds from their rooms. Absolute silence, they were sleeping like little angels. It took three hours for me to recover everything from the hiding places and get everything set up under and around the trees. Resting in my chair, I was overwhelmed taking in the site before me. "Thank you" a million times drifted to heaven through tears of gratitude.

I woke them early on Christmas morning to enjoy their gifts prior to attending church. After services our pastor asked us to stay behind for a few minutes. He handed us a large gift wrapped box with a card attached. Returning home there were more toys for each of them to enjoy. The card contained several $100.00 bills. I almost fainted. Everything was deeply appreciated especially the monetary donation. Our pastor never revealed who provided this gift, so I asked God to bless each parishioner. Prior to being reassigned to another parish one of the last things our pastor did was baptize each of the children.

After a couple of years it was obvious the children were here to stay. To celebrate, the kids and I decided to have a party. God sometimes has me doing things on a whim. This impromptu party was one of those times.

I soon figured out God had a reason for me doing this. He had scores of people lined up to help with future needs. And boy did the help roll in.

The guest list for the party was put together almost overnight. My neighbors and a couple of volunteers from a soup kitchen helped to organize the entire event. Food, soda, snacks, chairs and tables were donated. We invited all the kid's school and neighborhood friends, with a couple of my friends invited as well. One friend working in the legal field asked if her new boss, a fellow military veteran could come as well. He and one of his sons came to the party, and our family was blessed with a new friend that day.

He serves as the president for a childrens' support program. In this position he has access to resources designed to help families in need. While everyone was having a good time, my two youngest started what I call "clowning", running around without paying attention to what they were doing. Being a veteran he was quite familiar with military drill and ceremony commands. Without missing a beat, I called both children to ATTEN-TION and gave the command PARADE-REST. They immediately complied. My friend looked at them in amazement. The little ones were only four and five years old, both executed these commands flawlessly. He then looked at me and just fell out laughing. I explained to him that I had to go with what I know. Drill and ceremony commands work for me.

A few days later he called wanting to come by the house to see if there was anything he could do to help with the children. He also brought a brochure outlining various programs available at a dance studio owned by a family member. All the children were invited to join dance teams at no charge to us. This was a way for the kids to have something productive to do while teaching them discipline and responsibility as a team member. She wanted to give them an outlet for their boundless energy. I was floored with the offer and readily accepted. This was a true gift, a blessing in disguise. An added bonus was that my friend volunteered to come and get the children allowing me a few precious hours of badly needed peace and quiet.

Within no time at all, their entire family embraced ours. His wife became the hugs and kisses mom, the soft place to land when the children were in trouble with me. She held them to very high standards keeping an eye on their progress. Each of their mothers became surrogate grandmothers to my little brood. They lavished love on them as if they were flesh and blood relatives. My friend's sons became big brothers, their daughter a playmate. The kids always had a great time while visiting with their family doing things I was unable to afford at that time. My little ones really started to blossom being embraced by so much love. I see God's hand in this, but believe me, He was just getting started.

Many times our friend has come to our rescue. When my roof had several leaks all at once, he contacted a group that does repairs for low income families. A crew came out, replaced the entire roof, the broken back door, and installed smoke detectors.

The project was finished on Christmas Eve, God's gift for me that year. When the kids needed beds, he found a source for that as well. When my aging van was finally on its' last leg it needed to be replaced. He had a friend that worked for a car dealership and with their assistance I was to obtain a more reliable means of transportation.

As my youngsters were growing and doing well in school, more and more support materialized. The grade school children benefited from a local school supply program where children are given winter coats, hats, book bags, mittens, socks, shoes and school supplies. Another major blessing was the family discount at our local YMCA. Our charge was $10 a month, and I happily worked it into my budget. I took full advantage of several programs offered. Every Friday night I took the family to the Y's swimming pool and personally taught each of the kids to swim. Soon our outings became a family affair.

After a while my military vernacular with the kids became our normal conversation.

Whenever we were out in public people overhearing me speaking to the children seemed to be dumbfounded. Onlookers were quite sure they were hearing military commands, but were somewhat perplexed when they witnessed these little kids executing the commands. To a lot of folks this was something different, children **not** running around out of control.

As my youngsters were growing up, there were plenty of happy times, with many comical episodes. There was the Santa Claus knows everything you do, so if you want him to visit at Christmas, stay on his good list. The tooth fairy made regular deposits for lost baby teeth, and the Easter Bunny brought the fully loaded baskets of goodies. Birthdays were always celebrated with cakes and ice cream with loads of gifts. Often we were given tickets to events at a childrens' museum, the circus, carnival and a variety of other events. As they grew older, there were many other activities they were involved with, karate, little league softball, scouting, dance classes, performing arts, band/marching band, and every other educational ventures I could squeeze out of my budget.

My property is completely fenced in sitting on an acre of land. Over time I was able to get the children an eighteen foot above ground swimming pool, an eighteen foot enclosed trampoline, and sports equipment. Many supporters gave them basketballs, baseballs, roller skates, volley ball sets, tricycles, bicycles, and sleds for the winter. They were in no way deprived of a childhood. I have a treasure trove of pictures documenting the happiest times of our lives. Knowing they are loved, valued and important to this world helped them developed pride in who they are, and always to strive reaching higher goals.

I chose to raise these children different from my own childhood experience. Unlike my dad, I am retired and able to stay home full time with them. I never held the oldest child responsible for everything in the home, each one was responsible for their own behavior. This I hoped would avert resentment by not having the oldest child being held responsible for the younger children. Personal experience taught me that lesson. I wanted these children to love and support each other. It took many years for my siblings and me to get anywhere near that point. Sadly, they still see me as mean and bossy. I know it will take the fullness of time for them to understand how and why I got this way.

Once in a while I would see melancholy on the face of one or more of my little ones. They would be reluctant to tell me what was wrong, but I knew. I remembered that same emotion in my siblings from so long ago. Someone was missing from their lives. When those moments occurred, I stopped whatever I was doing and addressed the issue with them. Holding them in my lap close to my heart, I did my best to assure them they are deeply loved and no matter what life had in store for them I would always love and be there for them. We remained that way until they were relaxed and wanted to go play.

JUST BEING KIDS

Having a large back yard had its advantages. Over the years it was transformed into a busy playground. Many of their friends would join them in the swimming pool or playing on the trampoline. Watching from my kitchen window it warmed my heart to watch them having so much fun, enjoying life without a care in the world. During the summer the kids liked to have BBQs. The aroma of meats and vegetables on the grill delighted the senses. We enjoyed eating outdoors in the fresh air sitting around the picnic table. While we ate the kids would be busy telling me all about their new discoveries, a fallen bird nest, snakes they found while cutting the grass, or a doe with the mother deer spotted on the other side of the fence. They were growing and discovering the world around them. After a long day of play they often resembled little dirt balls. Not wanting dirt tracked inside the house I had them use the water hose to rinse off before coming inside.

On nights with clear skies we would take the telescope outside, set it on the tripod and scan the universe. Once they swore there were smiling faces with men on the moon. Every now and again Venus or Jupiter came into view being visible just before dawn. Passing aircraft with blinking colored lights were exciting to watch. Several times they thought flying saucers were coming to invade earth. Every 4th of July we set the lawn chairs in the yard to watch the neighborhood fireworks. I will always cherish the memory of seeing their little faces light up with squeals of delight hearing the booming sounds and watching the colorful displays. When they were a little older a family friend bought fireworks and taught them to safely set them off.

On a grocery shopping trip I realized the children assumed food was grown right there in the store. Remembering my aunt's farm and all the vegetables she grew, I realized it was time to plant our own garden. The next day we dug out a sizable patch of grass to grow vegetables. I bought several types of seeds and the garden was underway. Every day they were excited to see the progress of the "food" growing. Starting as tiny shoots poking through the soil to harvest was fascinating to the children. Before long we were picking the okra, green beans, lettuce, onions, tomatoes, and turnip greens we would eat for dinner. The corn didn't make it, the local squirrels had already dined on them prior to being ready to harvest.

Growing up the kids would often say amusing things. When the youngest was about six years old, it was announced at dinner one night that God was on holiday skiing in the Swiss Alps. This was said as a matter of fact with a straight face. The other kids and I lost it. So I asked this obviously precocious child who was in charge of the universe while God was on holiday. The reply, His second in command. OK. I guess that works. Another child, after visiting a museum and seeing the dinosaur section later asked my dad if he had a pet dinosaur when he was a kid. My dad pondered the question for a moment and replied that yes he was old, but not quite THAT old.

On another occurrence one of my bright children wanted some expensive name brand footwear. The cost was beyond the limits of my budget. It was explained to me this brand of shoes had amazing powers increasing the intelligence of anyone that wore them. Funny, I never heard that on the news. So we made a deal, if the usual run of the mill unimpressive grades were brought up to a solid B, I would buy the shoes. If these shoes were that miraculous I would love to have a genius in the family. A couple of weeks later the report card consisted of the same average grades, the shoes never made it home.

Several times one or the other would try selling me a tall tale about how they found themselves in trouble with me. Realizing the story I was being told didn't make sense, I did what I had previously done when my soldiers tried this same tactic. While they were explaining their story I took out my hand mirror and started checking my forehead. After a few seconds I stopped and asked if they saw the word "sucker" written across the front of my head. I told them that if they saw the word there to continue, if not, let's get to the truth of the matter.

Sometimes the kids got into minor mishaps at school with the excuse that some friend "made" them do it. I explained to that wayward child I sometimes couldn't get them to do things, but they were free to move to their friend's house and continue being manipulated to do things they knew better than. The point being is if you can mind your friend, feel free to move to their house and let their family feed you and pay your bills. If you decide to stay here, you need to rethink following the advice of someone else instead of thinking for yourself. You know the distinction between right and wrong and the ability to make choices for yourself. They understood the point.

There were times I felt overwhelmed caring for so many children. Again I question my sanity. Twice feeling at the end of my rope, God gently readjusted my thinking. Both times I thought I heard the kids up after bed time. Listening at their doors there was complete silence. Peeking in each of their rooms, all I saw was little angels fast asleep. The message placed in my mind was to protect these innocent little souls. Quietly standing there, God filled me with compassion and love for these little ones. With renewed strength I knew I could continue.

As the kids grew older they became curious about the medications I take. Hiding medicine in plain site was a favorite way for me to keep things away from them. Putting my pain killers in the frozen broccoli bag or a bag of carrots was ingenious. Not liking these vegetables meant anything in there was safe. One time, the oldest child was inquisitive about the chlorella food supplements I take every day. To keep the kids from bothering them I attached a warning label to the package indicating that if young boys took the supplement it would cause their private parts to shrink to the size of a peanut, girls would grow beards. This bluff worked like a charm. None of them ever bothered the supplements to find out if this was true or not. Smart move. Some of my friends were visiting and found this incident to be particularly amusing.

LESSONS FROM THE OLD SCHOOL

As a child from my generation obedient children was the rule not the exception. We were instructed from a very young age to say "please" and "thank you". Often we were told that children were to be seen, but not heard. In other words, you speak when spoken to. You understood to not interrupt adults in conversation with each other. Parents taught their children these manners as a way of respecting others and being grateful for things we were given. This is the practice I used with my young ones.

As an adult I can look back and appreciate the discipline my generation grew up under. Adults were respected by children and most of society helped and valued each other. Teachers were well regarded with complete autonomy over their classrooms. Using a ruler to whack the open hand of an unruly child was business as usual. Neighbors were expected to corrected a child caught doing something wrong. That same neighbor, after a serious tongue lashing would march you home to tell your parents what you were caught doing. And oh my Lord, you got it again from your parents. Trust me, being grounded was the least of your worries. An all day lecture concerning your wicked ways leading you straight to hell was followed by a butt tearing.

Whining or crying to get your way never worked. Parents told you to stop crying or they would give you something to actually cry about. This statement was reinforced with a hand getting ready to remove their belt. Translation: you are about to get your butt warmed up. We quickly learned that a hard head could result in having a soft behind. Pouting didn't work either, you were told to pull your lip in before you trip over it. We learned parents had eyes in the back of their head watching everything you were doing. We were informed, sometimes quite painfully, that adults really weren't born yesterday and money didn't grow on trees. Meaning: there wasn't a snowball's chance in hell of getting that desired "want", or we were informed that all the people in hell want ice water. A phrase we often heard was "give me drowned" and "I want went with him". My all time favorite response will always be "how does it feel to want"?

It is my opinion that some of the old school ways of discipline were far more effective than the "give the kid whatever they want method" that I see with a few parents today. As my youngsters were growing up, I relied on the old school, tried and true discipline that shaped my generation. They learned when I said no to something that **NO** was the final answer. It did not mean come back later to try again. Smart mouthing a teacher or any adult resulted in me taking that child back to that person and having the child apologize for their rude behavior. Lying and stealing were deadly sins. Along with being grounded they had to write a couple hundred lines of "I will not lie or steal." This was designed to lock in their mind this behavior was unacceptable and would not be tolerated. Writing the sentences helped improve their penmanship. Two birds -- one stone.

The kids knew when we were out in public be it church, a museum, or the zoo, if they acted out I would correct them on the spot. There was no such thing as waiting until we got home. The military taught me to correct a situation right on the spot, later may be too late for the lesson to be understood.

I had an arsenal of correcting methods. When away from home my two most effective methods were to either grab them by the shoulder where there is a sensitive nerve near the neck. A little pressure is applied and the pain halts whatever unconstructive behavior the child is doing. To onlookers it appeared I was gently restraining the child. Method two was to grab the head digging my finger nails in halting unacceptable behavior. To the bystander it appeared I was just holding onto the child. Noticing their bedroom door was closed when they left for school, I explained the door needed to remain open for air circulation. This directive went unheeded. I warned them that if they closed the door again I would remove it all together. Testing me on this issue was such a bad idea. The next day they closed the door, I removed it. Problem solved. Eventually the kids learned and understood my directives.

Often in a restaurant they would see children running around being a nuisance to waiters or other guests. I told mine that if they moved a muscle I would knock them completely out. Seeing my fist got the point across. I explained to them that running around restaurants or any other public place is rude as well as dangerous. Someone could be injured or cause injury to others. Often our waitress complemented my kids for being so well behaved and gave them a free dessert for their admirable behavior. This pleased me and delighted the children. Good behavior can have special rewards.

COVERT OPERATIONS

As time went on other parents would be amazed to see how well behaved my children were. I explained this was due to early training teaching them to be respectful and responsible for their actions. Sometimes mothers asked if I could come over to train their children. I smiled but politely declined explaining I had my own little ones to raise. Other mothers complained that they couldn't get their children to wash dishes, make their beds or clean their rooms. Some would indicate they had to call their child four or five times to get the child to empty the trash or do some other chore. Most of the time the parent decided to avoid an argument choosing to do the chore instead of insisting their children do it. Some of their children watched TV or played video games instead of doing homework. I was questioned as to why I didn't have these issues with my kids.

Asking the parent if they started teaching their child to do chores while they were growing up revealed the problem. The answer was usually "no". I explained that adjusting their child's behavior is not as difficult as they think. To regain control, the parent needed to change the playing field.

Hopefully these suggestions helped. I explained that telling the child who doesn't want to wash the dishes it's OK as long as they don't eat. If they don't eat, there aren't any dishes to wash. Not cooking until the kitchen is cleaned is an excellent incentive to get that chore done. It worked out very well around here. The hungrier they got, the faster their chores got done. If they don't want to make the beds, no problem, strip everything off the bed down to the bare mattress. Problem solved, especially in cold weather. If they don't want to clean their rooms, not a problem, do it yourself. Go in their room with a clean trash bag [or two] gather everything from the floor, under the bed, behind the dresser or other unauthorized places and put these items in the trash bag(s). Place the bag(s) in a safe place and let the child know since they couldn't clean their room you gladly did it for them. If they don't want to clean the bathtub, no problem, don't use these facilities. Let them go out in the yard, rinse off with the garden hose to clean the funk off their bodies. When they don't want to clean the toilet tell them to take a shovel out to the back yard, dig a hole, do their business and cover it back up. Unplugging the TV until all homework is done encourages completion of that task and set a definite time for TV. Extra TV or video game time can always be used as a special reward for good behavior. For the child who wants to ignore you when calling them, just go to where they are. If they are watching TV, turn it off, if playing a video game, take it from them. My youngsters soon learned if I turned the TV off, it stayed off until hell froze over. Bed time was bed time. All TVs and other electronic devices were turned off at the assigned time. The weekend had relaxed rules allowing them to stay up later. Granted, this sounds a little harsh, but very effective. Discipline taught my children responsibility and rules are in place for a reason. The child that is never held to any standards may never develop any.

It has been my experience that doing everything for children never teaches them how to do it for themselves. Yes, they will make mistakes, we all do, but that is how we learn what to do as well as what not to do. No one at age eighteen magically acquires a sense of responsibility. Character is built day by day, challenge by challenge. When faced with real life situations, the child could be lost having never developed the skills to think for themselves. All of this was implemented with mine from the day they came to my home. They quickly learned I say what I mean and mean what I say. These methods I refer to as my civilian version of covert operations or "Black Ops".

A time or two I was criticized by the way I parented my youngsters. I let those folks know if I *successfully* did my job now, the law and other authorities won't have to do it later. I love these children enough to be "hard core" when correcting unacceptable behavior. This I would do by any means necessary to accomplish the mission.

While still quite young, the kids assumed all parents were like me. As they grew older, imagine their surprise to discover a lot of their friend's discipline was seriously lacking in their home. Some of those same friends were in trouble with the law at a young age. Not allowing mine to follow along with every weird fad popular at the time had challenges. With grooming it was acceptable for girls to wear braids in their hair. However, it was mandatory for young men to maintain a short [military style] haircut. I explained this was necessary so that I could see and monitor what they were thinking. Of course the males wanted to look like their friends wearing a wild mass of hair on their heads, a no-go in my home. As a compromise I let their barber cut designs in their hair that actually looked nice. Teaching them that standing out in a positive way, and avoiding the negative crowd is what gets them noticed in life.

CHERISHING THE MEMORIES

It's very late at night and I'm still recalling memories of the adventures with the kids while they were just little tykes. Earlier in the day while cleaning out a closet I found a box I stored away many years earlier. Opening the box stopped me in my tracks. Inside were long forgotten memories of the kids while they were growing up, band schedules for their concerts, art objects, report cards and certificates of achievement honoring their accomplishments along the way. Handmade Christmas tree ornaments, Valentine's Day cards, and dried flowers saved from my birthday gifts were all intact. Several wallet-sized class pictures surprised me, were they ever really that young and innocent? At the very bottom of the box was a pillow I made for one of the kids. The angel I embroidered on it was to help the child sleep knowing there was protection from all harm and frightening things.

If only I could go back in time to once again kiss those dirty little faces, watch them playing in the bath tub or tickle their feet before going to sleep. I would give anything to hear them laughing and playing outside or to stand at the door watching them sleeping peacefully.

WHERE WE ARE TODAY

My children are all grown up and out on their own. I feel blessed and honored that God entrusted me with helping to shape their characters at a very young age. My journey with them is by far the most rewarding experience of my life. With them safely grown I can finally say NAILED IT! Each has graduated from high school. Two have graduated from college, two are in the Air Force with the rest preparing for civilian careers. None have been in prison, gangs, drugs or alcohol.

It is my prayer that as they go through life they each remember the lessons I instilled in them, being kind and gracious reflects from your soul, honesty and integrity are your most valuable credentials, and helping others is how you pay it forward to all those that helped you along the way. Most importantly, never let others define who you are. Develop your own character by thinking for yourself and deciding who you want to be. To say I'm proud of each of you is an understatement.

While writing and recalling how this journey began I am in awe as to how each piece of God's plan fell into place with perfect precision as my aunt predicted it would. God had prepared me all along with significant events in my life. Taking responsibility for my siblings taught me responsibility and child care, my aunt instilled spiritual qualities opening my heart to have compassion, and military training taught me endurance in the face of adversity. Each event strengthened me for the next step along my journey.

In my senior high school year book I remember a statement one of my teachers wrote. She looked at me for a moment and wrote "Give to the world the best you have and the best will come back to you". Being 17 years old, I didn't fully grasp the meaning. I never forgot the saying, and I believe it was always in the back of my mind.

Of all the unit patches I wore during military service one stands out as having a clear message. It read "Follow Me". Upon reflection, that was a message from God. Having blind faith going into the unknown can be frightening. I had to just trust, follow His lead, and He navigated me safely through the most troubling waters. With my hand in His, we walked this rocky road together.

Maybe, just maybe, I can go back into retirement. However, I will wait to see if God has yet another mission in mind. If so, I will carry out my new orders and soldier on.

Printed in the United States
By Bookmasters